Postcolonial Africa

Three Comparative Essays about the African State

Ben Wood Johnson

Series about international politics

TESKO

TESKO PUBLISHING

Pennsylvania

Published and printed in the United States of America by Tesko Publishing
(An Independent Publishing House)

Paperback format

ISBN-13: 978-1-948600-22-4 (paperback)
ISBN-10: 1-948600-22-6 (paperback

Cover design by Wood Oliver

Cover images
Copyright holder not raced. Any copyright concerned should be directed to
the address listed above. If contacted by the copyright holder, the publisher
would make the necessary adjustments and provide proper credits in
subsequent reprints. Cover illustration by Wood Oliver. For more
information about the author, visit his website at
www.drbenwoodjohnson.com

To my mother

Contents

vi *Contents*

Preface

AFRICA HAS AN EXTENSIVE HISTORY of colonization. But few people understand the nature of that history. This book elaborates on the continent's colonial past. The focus is on the sub-Saharan region.

Since 2015, a new reality has set in across Africa. A virulent disease (Ebola) led to a health crisis in various States. Most observers thought the ramifications of the outbreak would affect the continent for years to come.

To this day, there is a sense of uneasiness in Africa. Although the pandemic itself had been contained, there is a sentiment that it is not over. Many States live under the fear of a possible Ebola resurgence.

The Ebola disaster was a regrettable chapter in Africa's history. For years, the continent was making progress. The future is murky now, although it is not all gloomy; there is hope for the continent.

This text is not about the Ebola per se. Instead, it outlines a series of essay, which I compiled a few years back. Considering the recent events that took place in Africa, I revisited the subject.

The book is not exhaustive. However, it relates views echoed by well-known scholars about Africa. It is a way to become familiar with the issues that marked (or that continue to mark) the African State since the postcolonial period. Despite its limits, this work is not a fruitless intellectual pursuit. In that spirit, I encourage you to read the text cover to cover.

Good reading!
Ben Wood Johnson, Ph.D.
Pennsylvania, USA
May 2020

Introduction

WHAT IF I TOLD you that Africa is moving in the right direction, would you agree with me? Perhaps you would hesitate. The reality is not that great in Africa right now. Even though many countries are doing well, we could not say the same for others. Most African States are struggling to address an array of issues.

At any rate, one could also make the case that Africa is better than, say, twenty years ago. Does this mean that the continent has mastered its most pressing problems? Perhaps not, I would say. There are rooms for adjustments.

Despite the preceding considerations, there is a distressing reality on the African continent. Few could deny it. Africa is laden with troubles. The most recent adversity almost ruined the continent. It was the Ebola outbreak.

Even though the plague subsided, the situation is still confusing in most states. There is a sense of uneasiness. What might explain Africa's difficulties? I am not sure that there is a clear answer. But we could examine the continent's colonial past to make sense of it all.

This book is a comparative analysis about Africa's history. It is a compilation of three short essays. The text explores pre-colonial Africa and the continent's post-colonial era.

This is a brief, but to the point, review of the continent's political history. But the manuscript does not delve in depth in the issues. It does not examine Africa's social reality.

This edition references several works, which provide insights about the origins of Africa's current struggles. If you would like to learn more about Africa's history, refer to the publications cited recurrently in the manuscript. You may consult other works to discover Africa further.

The book contains five chapters. They are short. But they provide a concise assessment of the issues that pervade on the African continent.

The first two chapters are introductory. They situate the debate. They set the stage for the arguments I point out in the manuscript. These chapters outline recent events in Africa. They explore the Ebola spate, the effects of wars, conflicts, economic initiatives, politics, ecological problems, and security-related issues.

Chapter 3 outlines a snappy, but to the point, picture of the African State. It assesses similarities in the views offered by several authors. They include, but are not limited to, Crawford Young, Mahmood Mamdani, and Jeffrey Herbst.

Chapter 4 features an essay about the process of democratization in Africa. It explores the nature of elections and the rise of authoritarian regimes. The chapter assesses how democracy shaped Africa's political landscape. It reflects on the extent of progress and the limits of democratic reforms in many states since the early 1990s. The chapter assesses arguments that debate how democracy developed on the continent since the independence and until the Cold War.

Chapter 5 relates the extent to which state structures and other institutional legacies from the colonial era played a role in regime outcomes, conflicts, and development initiatives in Africa. The chapter relates how African individuals were groomed to rule on behalf of the colonial regime.

Chapter 6 examines the past, the present, and the future of the continent. It surveys the extent of colonialism during the post-colonial era. The chapter revisits efforts designed to achieve economic progress, development, political stability, and other efforts.

Chapter 7 provides a summary of the issues debated throughout the book. It relates the most salient questions echoed in the text. The book ends with a closing section. That segment includes a bibliography, an index, and a brief bio. It also features a list of my other works.

PART 1

The African Continent in
Recent History

CHAPTER 1

Africa from a Historical Lens

AFRICA HAS AN INTRIGUING history. That olden time, I must admit, is not glorious. It is a history of struggles; it is a history of sacrifice.

In recent decades, many African States sprung forward on the road of development. Still, things are not that great for the continent. There is a need to review important facets of the African

State. It is also central to revisit the continued struggle, which many nations begun experiencing over the last few years.

Africa's colonial past is omnipresent in the contemporary affairs of the motherland. Many countries face insuperable problems, including socio-political issues. These hurdles reflect a past that does not want to go away.

Africa's problems, I would also argue, are on par with the era of colonial domination. This is so even though many states gained their freedom. To this day, several African countries struggle to claim (or even to preserve) their own identity. The problem is that they develop in a world dominated, at least economically and geopolitically, by former colonial powers.

Until the late 1990s, many African States had regimes that mirrored the continent's colonial epoch. For ordinary Africans, social mobility was a distant dream. The reality was even more complicated for some states.

Despite having, what many consider, significant natural resources, poverty was (perhaps still is) rampant across Africa. A new form of *elitism* had replaced the old class of *European Bourgeoisie*. Nothing had changed (at least not drastically) after an era of hasty schemes for freedom and national independence. Several years after declaring their political autonomy, most African States were still under some form of political tutelage. Others were under foreign patronage.

Certainly, new African regimes had replaced the old European model of governance. But many of these new political factions were corrupt at their core. Many new leaders expressed no genuine desire to see the motherland prosper.

Assessing the Role of Africans

Could we blame African leaders for the ills of the continent? I am not sure that there is a definite answer. What is not debatable is that Africans played a role, although not substantial, some might say, in the continent's troubles. But that role could not be more obvious during the post-colonial era. Africans themselves ruled Africa; at least, it was the case on the surface.

It is true that native Africans, at least in most cases, led the new regimes, which replaced the old ones. However, the situation on the ground remained similar to the reality that existed during the colonial era. South Africa, for instance, was still a bifurcated state. Apartheid, just as during the time of European domination, was the *De Facto* condition under which many people in South African felt forced to live.

In various African regions, achieving progress was an elusive goal. Few leaders bothered to aim for it. Some regimes had little or no appreciation for the notion of democracy. As a result, undemocratic regimes were legion in various parts of Africa. The remnants of the old form of administrations collided with any movements toward democracy and sustainable development.

Achieving progress in Africa seemed impossible. For a long time, anything that resembled positive changes were often met with a notable amount of resistance from both internal and external forces. One had a sense that Africans did not want to break free from the old customs of the colonial era. Despite that dim reality, it was also obvious that the old masters did not want to emancipate their former captives. It was a dangerous game of prestidigitation.

Despite the dreary days of the 1980s and even throughout the 1990s, there was a sense that things were changing for the better in Africa. Several African countries pulled away from the problems, which, some might say, held them back for several years (if not decades) after their independence. There was a sense that a new Africa was sprouting out of the arid lands of the embattled continent.

Africa in a Post-Ebola Era

The Ebola health crisis had a psychological effect on many Africans. In parts of Africa, many people are still afraid of a potential outbreak. Few people could deny that state of constant panic throughout the continent.

What might explain that new reality? The answer is not clear. Some might say that is a sense of scare from infectious diseases. Another reality is also worth noting.

The view in most western corners is that the African continent did not do away with some of the issues, which dominated its past. Recurring problems, such as political instability, economic stagnation, poverty, and anti-democratic regimes, to name a few, continue to plague many nations.

There is cautious optimism for Africa these days. There is also a growing sense of fear. Such anxieties are not necessarily the result of exaggerated predilections for the continent. It is as though disaster is just around the corner.

Until the year 2014, Africa seemed in good shape. Most observers agreed that the continent was making progress in various domains. Things were changing for the better. Then, something terrible happened. It was the Ebola outbreak.

The Ebola scare was a calamity for many Africans. Countless people perished from the disease. The outburst wreaked havoc in many states. Countries like Guinea, Liberia, and Sierra Leone were the most affected.[1] That new reality, some could argue, set the continent back.

Before the epidemic, Africa, as a continent of course, was doing relatively well. Several states were doing outstandingly great. When it comes to good governance, others were in great health.

---

[1] The Center for Disease Control and Prevention notes that many people died from the Ebola outbreak. Approximately 11, 325 people perished. See the CDC's website for more information. (Center for Disease Control and Prevention, 2020)

Most countries were heading on the path toward economic independence. This was significant considering the alternatives. It was great to see many African States, some of which had a history of struggle, living up to the expectations of their citizens.

The reality on the ground was also improving from a political lens. Many states held elections regularly. Africa, often, had not been in the news because of successive military coups or stories about genocides or starvations. Africa, as a whole, was—perhaps once again—a thriving continent.

This is not to say that everything was rosy. There were significant problems. Many of these hurdles engulfed the continent for the worse.

Before the Ebola crisis, not everything was great in Africa. Real democracy and the adhesion to universal principles about human rights were not perfect in many places. It is also worthy of note that peace and security improved in various regions. This was a huge affair, considering that the continent experienced wars, famine, environmental disasters, and other problems, for example since the 1980s and all the way through the 1990s.

There were encouraging developments on the economic front. Such trends were obvious throughout the continent. Some of these states had a history of economic stagnation. Things, to reiterate, were starting to change for the better.

Since the new millennium, various African countries enjoyed a relatively healthy and stable economy. A handful of states had consistently ranked among the world's healthiest economies. Things were not bad at all for Africa; at least in certain domains.

A Rosy Picture

It is unquestionable that Africa had a rough start. Soon after declaring their independence, many countries faced significant problems. New African leaders needed to address them at once. But many of them failed to do so within a reasonable timeframe. Of course, we could agree to disagree about why that was the case.

Notwithstanding our potential disagreements, we must reckon that the African environment was degrading at an alarming pace. Domestic problems and other issues represented a major impediment for the progress of various states.

But there were internal complications, which made it nearly impossible for new leaders to make a tangible difference on their land.

Who is to blame for Africa's troubles? Answers are not clear. The trend in most circles is to blame Africans themselves. Could we say that Africans are the only culprits? I am not sure.

It would be *naïve* to overlook the role that external forces or other extraneous reasons played in making it difficult (if not impossible) for most African leaders to uplift their country. Vital factors, such as, globalization, privatization, and external interests had a negative effect on the continent. Despite it all, many states tried to achieve sustainable development. Still, the future was uncertain for many others. That reality had a negative impact on Africa as a whole.

Understanding Africa's Colonial Past

In trying to understand Africa, let us consider the following questions. Why Africa's future is uncertain? Why the continent's reality is bleak? Why efforts undertaken by some states to change their reality are fading away? We might find satisfying answers only by examining the continent's colonial past.

It is incontrovertible that colonialism had a significant impact on the African continent. What might explain that reality? A likely explanation is that state structures and other institutional legacies from the colonial era continued to play an important role in creating predetermined regime outcomes, such as conflicts, wars, and other economic or political ills. These realities hampered development in many states.

Even though the outlook had been improving on various fronts, the future of states, such as Nigeria, Senegal, Mali, Liberia, and Sierra Leone, is bleak. A lot is at stake for those states. The anxiety from the Ebola itself could have negative impacts on the continent for years to come.

While the issues previously outlined are worth considering, when assessing the immediate future of Africa, there is more to the continent than meets the eye. To understand Africa's present and even its immediate future, there is a need to reassess its past. There is a need to reexamine the continent's colonial history.

CHAPTER 2

Africa's Political History

BEFORE WE DELVE in the colonial past of the African continent, let us revisit its recent history. Some observers would have you believe that things have always been bad in Africa. Mainstream media in most developed countries, including France, Great Britain, and the United States, often depict a dying Africa. But is that the only picture the continent has to offer? I would say no.

True, the ravaging effects of poverty and other social ills in many African countries can be alarming. Various news outlets display these problems. Local newspapers across the world regularly draw attention to the plights of African immigrants. The continent's difficulties are often the highlights of news websites and blogs.

I could not argue that Africa, as a whole, is doing well right now. There are significant issues on the continent. Some of them need attentions. Vital problems are still ravaging the African people. But there is a lack of genuine concern for Africa.

What is the real story in Africa? Are the situations dire there than most would admit? I do not have an answer.

What is obvious is that few people are likely to relegate the African social [or political] reality in the most genuine manner. Few people are apt to explain Africa's difficulties accurately. Some might say this is the reason views are likely to diverge about the nature of the problems that the African State faced.

Not too long ago, the consensus was that the prospects were somber for many African countries. Most observers predicted a bleak future for the continent. These concerns, I would admit, were not baseless.

A Depressing Future

Over two decades ago, Africa was afflicted with all sorts of problems, including ethnic disputes, wars, diseases, and political upheaval. In parts of the land, economic advancements were scarce, if not stagnant. Other issues, including contagious and deadly diseases (that is, HIV/AIDS, Malaria, Dysentery, Yellow Fever, and Chikungunya, to name a few), plagued the continent. Recurrent problems, such as annual drought, domestic conflicts, poverty, and corruption hindered any possibility for long-term progress.

Despite the reality of the African State, no one knew exactly what was going on in Africa. A few scholars argued that it was nearly impossible to assess the real reason certain African countries could not progress. But some observers pointed out that grasping the history of the continent was essential, if not necessary. It was the best way to understand the extent of the problems that pervaded in certain regions. They argued that the unprecedented turmoil, which characterized the continent back then, was not an act of God.

Crawford Young, for instance, is among those who thought that the past was infringing on the future of the continent. In the book titled *The African Colonial State in comparative perspective,* which came out in 1994, Young contends that Africa's failure to develop was by design.[2] The author hints that the colonial experience shaped Africa. Colonial powers manipulated states' social structures and institutions to benefit their own interests.

While not everyone agreed on the true nature of Africa's problems, many observers are likely to explore the issues from a narrow mindset. A popular viewpoint is that Africa's problems are intrinsic to the continent. The African people contributed to their own problems, they say. This is to say that Africans played a major role in fostering a climate of stagnation in their countries. Put another way, African peoples are responsible for the reality of the continent.

---

[2] Young, C. (1994). *The African colonial state in comparative perspective.* New Haven, CT: Yale University Press

I do not agree with the previous viewpoint. In my view, Africa is the victim of the economic proclivities of colonial powers. Thus, Africa or Africans alone should not be held responsible to the tumults of the continents. We must consider other factors.

The Role of External Agency

Crawford Young notes that the African problem is a direct result of colonialism. He points out that we could understand Africa from three historical prisms: (1) a pre-colonial era, which was experienced by the interference of external forces; (2) a colonial period, which geography and colonial expansion heavily dominated; and (3) a post-colonial period. This era became the trademark of influences by agency.[3]

Young further argues that external agency played a minimal role in Africa. For him, the continent's problems, if we could refer to it that way, was a local product. But I would content that colonial powers mostly influenced local

---

[3] The term "agency" denotes the notion of foreign influence in the domestic issues of a country.

institutions. In fact, it is patent that colonial powers themselves put these institutions in place. Perhaps it was a well-crafted ploy by the colonial regimes to leave their imprint on the African continent for years to come.

In the previously cited publication (*The African Colonial State in Comparative Perspective*), Young notes that institutions and domestic issues, namely population density, played a big role in conflicts. These social realities, according to Young, stifled positive initiatives toward sustainable development and growth.

While I share facets of Crawford Young's historical assessment of the African continent, I am convinced that colonialism played a more important role in shaping local attitudes toward the motherland. If the African peoples themselves were to be held responsible for their own misfortunes, perhaps it would be because they were taught to put the needs of the homeland last. I could not absolve colonial powers in trying to turn Africa into a wasteland.

A Plethora of Issues

After World War II, an array of African colonies got their independence from various European countries, namely France, England, and Belgium. But these gains, some might say, came with a hefty price. Since the 1950s and, arguably, until the 1990s, most African States experienced important issues, including political problems, environmental hurdles, and social upheavals. Who deserves the blame?

Many observers, chiefly western political scientists, have long debated the reasons African countries seemed entangled in a stagnant state of affairs. The pervading belief in the Western world is that many states did not move in the right direction because of political unrests and other social complications. Is there any truth to that viewpoint? I am not sure how to frame the debate satisfactorily. Here is why...

Views often diverged about the cause of Africa's troubles. Popular presumptions center on the role of culture, state structures, and other institutional legacies. I am not sure that this work alone could change that dynamic.

The argument often echoed in the literature is that during the postcolonial era, Africa changed for the better. It became independent. The continent was no longer under the scope of external forces. Is there any truth in that assertion? I would say no.

It is debatable that Africa, as a continent of course, has ever been independent. Some observers might say that most African countries are always under external dependence. This could not be more obvious after many states declared their independence.

We could make the case that the social structures that were put in place by the former colonial masters set up a social labyrinth for new African leaders. Newly settled governments could not lead their country without relying on foreign supports, financial aids, or political guidance. Those that did not rely on foreign backing or foreign dicta often became the victim of spectacular military coups. Those coups, in turn, often yielded despotic regimes. Therefore, we could make the irrefutable argument that colonial regimes [or colonial structures] long before the independence determined Africa's future.

The most virulent remnants of colonialism plagued the African State. They did so for many years after the independence. Institutional structures or the effects of foreign agency led to a constant need for anti-democratic regimes. Those regimes, in turn, contributed to increasing the likelihood of conflicts in various parts of the region.

Some observers believe that after the independence, there had been an alarming antidemocratic trend in Africa. Almost regularly, a regime would experience a coup d'état. A power-hungry group would replace that regime. That group would later suffer a similar fate.

Here and there, there would be mass killings. Other forms of problems, namely a rise in state brutality, characterized Africa. It is indisputable that poverty was a major feature of the newly created African State.

Throughout the 1980s, Africa was in a dire shape. The continent was marred with wars (mostly civilian conflicts), drought, diseases, and poverty. Political turmoil and other types of social morasses led to an incommensurable period of social instabilities on the continent. It is unquestionable that this reality hampered development in many African States all the way through the new millennium.

In making the previous concessions, I would admit that Africans are not saints. I would not refute the notion that African leaders seemingly played a role in worsening the ills of the continent. But arguing that they are the only culprits would be misguided.

While I take issues with some of the arguments that Crawford Young offered about the reason Africa is in such a dire state, I would not dismiss the role of external agencies in destroying the African continent though. I would also argue the story of Africa is more complex than that. Let us explore the continent's political history to make sense of it all.

PART 2

Essay One: The Bula Matari

CHAPTER 3

The Nature of African Politics

AFRICA IS AN ENORMOUS continent. It contains several states, many of which are dependent and self-governed; at least, this is so in theory. Tordoff (2002) notes that, Africa, as a continent, is vast; it is also diverse. Africa is comprised of more than 50 independent states. Even so, understandings about Africa's political history (or the origins of the African State itself) are not that concise. Africa is a painfully enduring puzzle, Englebert (2000) notes.

The nature of African politics and the way the African State itself developed are not well understood in Political Science. What is certain is that: "Africa's fifty-four states are the product of conquest and separation, amalgamation and continuity" (Chazan et al, 1999, p. 5).

The present essay explores several works authored principally by prominent scholars about African politics. The focus is on three works, which feature views echoed by Crawford Young, Mahmood Mamdani, and Jeffrey Herbst. These authors present compelling arguments about the origins of the African State.

Some of the views outlined by the previously mentioned authors are conciliatory and, at times, overlapping. Of course, there are striking differences in their arguments. Nonetheless, Mahmood Mamdani offers a more complete explanation of the origin of the African State. This author lays out the most convincing [perhaps the most irrefutable] claims about creating the African Statehood. Let us explore their argumentations.

Crawford Young and the African State

Crawford Young argues that the African State itself was not a direct product of colonialism. The African collective existed as a state long before it was wiped out and perhaps reinvented because of colonialism. Overtime, however, there was a shift in the reality of the continent.

Young (1994) divides the colonial epoch in three periods. The first period consisted of the moment of conquest until World War I. According to the author, the goal was to "construct an apparatus of domination that would transform military (sometimes political) subordination into permanent rule" (Young, 1994, p. 10). That state was relatively peaceful and passive.

The second period consisted of interwar years. During that time, Africa experienced an awful external domination. This time was mainly marked by an era of consolidation. During that epoch, colonial domination was institutionalized, rationalized, and routinized (Young, 1994, p. 10). As the name suggests, it was an era of forced integration and forced assimilation to foreign cultures and ways of life.

The third [or the last] period was marked by an era of restoration. This moment in Africa's political history experienced a rise of African nationalism. It was also an era of struggle for sovereignty and the formal decolonization of the continent.

There is a need to grasp the arguments that Crawford Young echoed about the nature of the African State. In it lies a clue to understand the reason some African States are still in a difficult stage at this point in their history. Young argues that two facets characterize the African State itself. The first one is concerned with the state as a theoretical object. The second approach deals with the state as a macro-historical actor.

As a national object, the African State has eight crucial features: territory, population, sovereignty, power, law, the state as a nation, the state as an international actor, and the state as an idea. Within the context of a historical actor, the African State can be understood from six different angles or from six distinctive characteristics. They are as follows: hegemony, autonomy, security, legitimacy, revenue, and accumulation (Young, 1994).

The belief in most scholarly circles is that after the independence, African leaders inherited the Africa that was handed down to them. Young (1994) also argues that structures that had been put in place by Europeans still dictated the polity of the states. After the independence, the African State was condemned to reproduce the same ideals or the same institutions created by the Colonial State.

Although the state failed in other domains, such as legitimacy, autonomy, infrastructure, and accumulation of wealth for the people, to name a few, leaders were successful in building state power; they were good at the naked exercise of power.

Within the previously noted context, we could classify the essential features of the African State in the following manner: colonialism (also known as the Bula Matari), colonial differences between the British and the French, the impact of external influences in state affairs, state strength, and the changes that occurred in the states after World War II.

The Bula Matari

Mainly used as a metaphor, the term "Bula Matari" (he who crushes rocks) depicts an African State where the sheer brute force and the crushing power of Europeans were visible to the naked eyes. "The name of Bula Mata(r)i signified terror" (Young, 1994, p. 1). In this violent state of affairs, white domination became the trademark of imperial hegemony.

Bula Matari was the instrument that eased colonial dominance and white supremacy over the African State. This practice was mostly espoused by the Belgian. It was also used in the African Colonial State, that is, in the African colonies.

Young argues that Bula Matari was Omnipresent in the African State. The notion of Bula Matari itself became so engrained in the fundamental existence of the state that it had "a formidable capacity for its own reproduction across time and in the face of systematic efforts by new regimes to uproot prior forms and build new blueprints" (Young, 1994, p. 2). This new form of colonialism was the tool used by most Europeans, including the French, the British, and the Belgian, to impose "the superstructure of alien rule" (Young, 1994, p. 2). Per contra, it was a codeword for the superstructure of alien rule. After the independence, the African State continued in the same path of terror, Young (1994) noted.

Colonial Differences in Africa

Colonial Africa was characterized by a rigid colonial polity. When Europeans arrived on the continent, they had perfected colonialism. By then, the Colonial State was "a far more distinctive polity than its predecessors were (Young, 1994, p. 76).

State institutions were carefully crafted to subdue local communities. Young (1994) further notes that the British, the French, and the Belgian had a different colonial approach as opposed to the African State. Their philosophy about colonialism and white dominance varied. These distinctions also affected the African State unevenly. To sketch this assertion further, Young (1994) notes that:

"The colonizing states, despite sharing many fundamental attributes toward their newfound vocation of African domination and the

*societies on which they imposed their rule, also
had some differences in their own historically
shaped personalities as polities" (Young, 1994,
p. 79).*

Europeans carried out different strategies to
conquer Africa. They used settlers, charter
companies, military forces, signed treaties, and
missionaries as a means to widen their dominion
over the African State itself. In regions where the
climate was more temperate, for instance, white
settlers moved in greater number than in other
geographically challenged places.

The colonies that had more settlers enjoyed
more political privileges and power. Those
settlers feared the African elite. Europeans also
used different legal codes for Africans and
European settlers. Inequity was legion in the
colonial legal system, chiefly in the British and
French colonies.

Europeans used two sets of laws: one set of
laws for Africans and different laws for Whites.
The British used indirect rules to conquer Africa.
They used Africans to enforce their own rules,
that is, British rules. They also used traditional
African rules.

The French, on the other hand, had a different approach. They favored assimilation as a way to conquer the African State. They felt more threatened to traditional rules. They also worked to undermine those rules. For example, Uganda (West Africa), a British colony, had more educated elite.

The newly created African State was keen on getting enough revenues to strengthen its institutions. The state also sought revenue as a means to set up more control over the citizenry. To create revenue, the state "engaged in a ceaseless struggle with civil society to extract the resources necessary for performance of its other roles" (Young, 1994, p. 38).

The state used various strategies to create revenue. For example, they imposed taxes; they extracted minerals; they imposed forced labor.

Laws were imposed to make it illegal for Africans to be unemployed. Those laws favored Europeans, not Africans. People found it necessary to work almost gratis (free). Others were paid next to nothing for their labor. This strategy led to the bourgeoning of a Capitalistic economy, which also lead to capitalistic development of wealth.

Assessing External Influence

Young (1994) claims that external forces influenced state power. In theory, the state was independent. But in practice, the state had little or no sovereignty. From an internal perspective, state suffered from a chronic legitimacy problem.

On the one hand, state authority was limited to its subjects. On the other hand, state authority was tied to its capacities to exert that authority. Because of institutional constraints, states could not enjoy any sense of sovereignty. Young (1994) notes, "In the colonial polity no real *état de droit* existed to restrain its domination of subject society" (Young, 1994, p. 30).

The state enjoyed less sovereignty as well. In this case, "Power remains the most important currency of international affairs and most states are usually in no position to enforce their will against the opposition of others" (Young, 1994. p. 29). States had no power in institutional polity.

On the economic front, states had no relevance. Because of external influences, there was an accumulation of foreign currency in the state. This led to a shift from a local economy to a global economy. As a result, people no longer produced goods. They imported most of their food (Young, 1994).

The Cold War Effects

After the Second World War, the nature of the African States changed. Soon after the skirmishes officially ended, the African State was subjected to indirect rule at home. The state struggled to expand its hegemony on the land.

Often, power struggles and political incompatibilities brought about political upheaval, including military coups d'état as time went by. There was also a change from military to civilian rule. States tried to increase attention and legitimacy by stressing state-building initiatives. For example, after independence, states focused on building schools, roads, and infrastructures.

Understanding States Strength

Young (1994) contends the Colonial State was weak. It lacked sovereignty (Young, 1994). After the independence as well, states were successful at setting up their own power. Hegemony led to a need for security, which, in turn, led to an absurd accumulation of wealth and legitimacy.

The state security apparatus also led to hypertrophy (Young, 1994, p. 7). The author notes that the African State spent billions in armament, which led to a huge external debt. It led to unnecessary conflicts. As we go along in the debate, let us consider another approach to understanding the African State's recurring troubles.

Mahmood Mamdani and the African State

Mamdani depicts the African State from a different lens. He portrays the state as a new phenomenon within the context of a historical formation. He argues the Colonial State was different, but shared certain fundamental features in history (Mamdani, 1996).

Contrary to Crawford Young, Mahmood Mamdani argues that the colonial experiment led to a new African State. It was a state, which never existed before. The problem is that this new African State was also bifurcated.

The fundamental motive for creating this new state was the native question. Mamdani (1996) argues, "Direct rule was Europe's initial response to the problem of administering colonies" (Mamdani, 1996, p. 16). By contrast, "Indirect rule came to be the mode of domination over a 'free' peasantry" (Mamdani, 1996, p. 17).

Mamdani characterized the essential features of the African State in the following manner: there was a bifurcated state. There was direct and indirect rule. There was institutional segregation; there was territorial segregation. Thus, the African State itself was not a homogeneous entity.

The Bifurcated State

The term "bifurcated state" sketches two forms of power under a single ruling authority. The term also draws a dual approach to the form of colonization, which the European used over an indigenous majority in Africa. The Colonial State was a double-sided affair (Mamdani, 1996, p. 19).

Mamdani notes that the African bifurcated state was comprised of two forms of rules: a direct and an indirect ruling system. But as a whole, their impact could be incommensurable in the State itself.

Direct and Indirect Rule

In the direct ruling system, there was a single legal order. Direct rule was also a form of control on urban spaces (Mamdani, 1996, p. 18). This was the early response the Europeans devised to address administrative issues in Africa.

In the indirect ruling system, proxies, such as tribes and chiefs, exerted power on the population. Those proxies were accountable only to the Europeans. This control suggested a form rural tribal authority (Mamdani, 1996, p. 18). Indirect rule sketches out the means of domination the Europeans espoused over the peasantry.

As noted earlier, the British and the French had different strategies in Africa. This was also true when it comes to the rule they espoused. As opposed to the French, the British espoused a more hand-off approach.

The British were likely to recognize traditional authority. They were unlikely to disturb a preexisting authority, markedly if they were not threatening by it. For example, because of past colonial experiences, namely in Asia, the British favored a generalized decentralized despotism as their "practical answer to the native question" (Mamdani, 1996, p.18).

On this side of despotism, native authority was the decentralized arm of the Colonial State. They used pressure to compel free peasants into forced labor. The chiefs yielded much power over the peasantry. The British perception is that Chiefs could use "their customary powers to keep order and exact labor to help themselves along the way" (Mamdani, 1996, p. 56).

Indeed, they did just that. As a result, they helped maintained the status quo; they helped consolidate British rule on the African State.

The French, on the other hand, felt more threaten by large African States. They broke them up. Of course, they recognized local authority at some level. But there was less capitalistic development in the French colonies.

The French were more interested in assimilation. The British, on the other hand, favored traditional authority (in this case, ethnicity). The French favored their authority. It is also worthy of note that there was more racism in the British colonies.

Institutional Segregation

The term institutional segregation is referred to a form of segregation brought about by state institutions. Institutions were used as the primary means to separate between the natives and European settlers. This approach was grounded in a politically enforced arrangement of ethnic pluralism (Mamdani, 1996).

Within the context of the native question or problem, native institutions were heavily influenced by European norms, even though natives were territorially separated from white settlers. In the British colonies, there were two legal institutions. But institutions were set apart for different parts of the population, which resulted in apartheid. Because of the strategy of creating division within the state, apartheid was successful (Mamdani, 1996).

In institutional segregation, the natives were not forced to assimilate into a common type. This approach consisted of policies of institutional homogenization. It was a broader form of racial segregation. This approach was also a way of preserving native institutions, while meeting the labor demands of a growing economy (Mamdani, 1996).

Territorial Segregation

Territorial segregation was based on the territorial separation between the natives and European settlers. This was done mostly through ethnic disparities and cultural differences (Mamdani, 1996). This practice was normalized through state institutions.

Africans were removed from the city. They were forced into their homeland (known as well as African reserve). This form of segregation received supports from local Africans. Blacks, mostly women and children, were sent back home, while the men remained to work in the mining industry.

Europeans convinced Africans that such a set-up would benefit them. Africans would receive protection from abuse that could happen under direct rule, they said. Europeans further argued that modernization would damage traditions. As a result, Europeans could not buy African lands. The state could market and justify segregation under the promise of protection.

South Africa in particular had an industrialization problem. On the one hand, they needed labor. By contrast, they did not want Africans to remain in the city. They used forced removal as a means to mitigate that problem. It was also a strategy (or it was an institutional means) to reduce the possibility for African workers or city dwellers to demand services or better wages.

So far, we have examined the views expressed by Crawford Young. We also examined the arguments proposed by Mahmood Mamdani to understand the nature of the African State. To wrap up this discussion, let us consider the views echoed by Jeffrey Herbst.

Jeffrey Herbst and the African State

Jeffrey Herbst argues that the African State was characterized by its geography. Everything about the role of the state could become obvious by exploring its geographic descriptions. Just like Crawford Young, the author (Herbst) denotes three important periods about the African State.

They are as follows: pre-colonial, colonial, and postcolonial.

During the pre-colonial phase, the state was dominated by external reasons. Africa was made up of several large empires (Herbst, 2000). During the colonial stage, geography played a major role in shaping European influence on the African State itself. The continent began experiencing the rise of small city-states.

After the independence, agency was more prevalent on the continent. Through agency, institutions played a more prominent role in reinforcing colonial structures. According to Herbst (2000), the essential features of the African Colonial State include geography, weak state, population density, and state building.

Geography

Geographic description on the African continent led to a clear demarcation between the people and the land (Herbst, 2000). This reality led to a clear distinction between Africans and Europeans. Europeans built capitals in places separated from where Africans lived. They build cities and capitals near ports. Ports were important because they allowed for shipment of trades or other valuable items.

The African State is Weak

After the independence, the African State was considered weak. However, state weakness did not impede geographic boundaries. Borders still mattered in the African State (Herbst, 2000). The security apparatus were also weak.

It must be noted that this weakness was the result of Europeans agreement that they would not fight over Africa. As a result, they did not need a large military complex or apparatus. States could control and dominate with few people on the ground (Herbst, 2000).

Population Density

Population density was a major issue in the new African State. Many of the recently created states strived to set up control over resources rather than the land itself. Because there were fewer technologies, this reality had an enormous impact on agriculture. Back then, most African peasants relied on rain fed agriculture.

When lands were exhausted, people moved in different regions. In that sense, population density was a basic problem in the African State. This was an issue, which every new African ruler struggled to manage (Herbst, 2000).

State Building Issues

The African State engaged in efforts, which some political observers coined "state-building" initiatives. War and amassing wealth were directly related to state building initiatives. Many states needed the military to conquer the land. As a result, there was a need for people to take over the land and to collect taxes.

After the independence, there was a dilemma. The dynamic had changed. They had to decide whether to change border or to control ports. The effect of preserving the borders was that it legitimized the rulers (Herbst, 2000). As a direct result, the power of the colonial era remained the same even after the independence.

To avoid wars, many states decided not to change the border. They focused on controlling ports. The new leaders assumed that they could tax trade. States were also reluctant to tax the people. As a result, there were little inter-state wars. Until now, weak states remained an important flaw on the African continent.

Finding Common Ground

On what issues these authors mentioned in the preceding pages agreed. Mahmood Mamdani, Crawford Young, and Jeff Herbst suggest that through trial and error, the Europeans were able to instill their supremacy on the African State. Mamdani in particular argues that the British could fine-tune their approach to colonization in part because of their experience in Asia, namely in India.

To some extent, Young and Mamdani disagree whether colonization deeply changed the African State. By contrast, Young agree that a degree of bifurcation existed in the African State. He also echoes that such a split was present only between the British and the French with their imperial privileges.

For Young, colonization unquestionably changed Africa. Just like Herbst, Young (1994) recognizes that a state is a territorial entity. Young further recognizes the importance of population and the role of population density.

He argues, "A state that lost its population (or its territory) ceases to exist" (Young, 1994, p. 27).

Mamdani and Young share similar viewpoints about the notion of Bula Matari. But for Mamdani, African and European agency affected the African State. He argues that Bula Matari was the reason the African State itself existed.

Let me further emphasize that the Bula Matari remained in effect, even after the independence. The bifurcated state led to a breakdown of traditional power (Mamdani, 1996). Power was not backed up by traditions.

Examining Divergence

On what issues the authors disagree. The authors agree that colonialism had an effect on the African State. However, the explanations they provide are different. Herbst and Young coincide on the role of geography. As opposed to Herbst (2000), Young (1994) argues the territorial dimension of the state was determined, not by geography, rather by the bourgeoning emergence of a global scheme of states with precise boundary demarcations.

Crawford Young further notes, "Physical artifacts--boundary markets, even fences--represent territorial limits" (Young, 1994, p. 26). Essentially, the territorial boundaries of the African State shifted. Boundaries were personified by uninformed state agents, inanimate objects, and flags. Through these artifacts or via these symbolic outlines, states asserted their authority (Young, 1994).

While Herbst focuses on geography, Mamdani centers on the role of institutions. Herbst argues that geography played a significant role in the African State. But for Mamdani, institutional set up, which was the result of the bifurcated state, played a more prominent role in defining the essential characteristics of the African State.

Contrary to the other authors, Mamdani's perspective is more convincing. His approach stands out as a stunning departure from common beliefs about Africa, at least as a political entity. Mamdani's writings led to a change of model in African studies. This author put forth the notion that both Africans and Europeans played a role in destroying the African State.

Mamdani notes that certain structures that had been put in place by the Europeans lasted long after the independence. Those structures, he further points out, created disunity and division, which in turn led to policies and political frameworks that further undermined the African State. This view is in line with the assertion echoed in Young (1994, p. 6), *"Dominer pour servir,"* as a form imperial dominance on the Colonial State.

Mamdani notes that there were two African States within the African State itself. There was a state, which was governed by formal rules (as he put it, direct rules). There was also a state, which was governed by informal rules or indirect rules.

The indirectly ruled state was relegated to the whims of tribes through the means of institutional policies and practices. To this day, Africa is still plagued by this notion of tribalism. The notion of tribal rules remains the basis of hostility among the African people. This reality was common as both an internal and an external problem for the African State.

Mamdani refutes the notion that South Africa was exceptional. He argues that the South African experiment was refined over time. He also points out that the true origin of Apartheid was based on a "divide and conquer" strategy, which had been perfected by Great Britain and France over the course of time.

PART 3

Essay Two: African Democracy

CHAPTER 4

A Search for Democracy

WHEN ONE SPEAKS OF democracy or the process of democratization, what usually comes to mind is the idea of political stability or political freedom. The notion of political freedom is often associated with habitual organizations of free and fair elections. It is also believed that organizing free and fair elections may provide a snapshot of how democratic institutions, such as electoral institutions, work. But that is not always true for the newly created African State.

The African State often organizes elections. That does not necessarily mean that such elections are democratic in nature. Often, they are not democratic at all. In other words, the idea of democracy is elastic on the African continent.

Since the 1950s, there had been periodic organizations of elections in Africa. Excluding, that does not suggest that democracy in that part of the world is in good standing. These elections seldom depict a true picture about the nature of democracy across the continent.

After the independence, elections were just a way to legitimize a regime, which gained power through other means. While many African countries held regular elections, the outcomes of those elections created political environments where true democracy seldom thrived. In the newly created African State, elections are not always synonymous with democracy.

The term democracy itself does not have a universal understanding in political theory. Most scholars would agree that African democracy is even murkier than that viewpoint. The concept is not well understood from a Western lens.

Lindberg (2004) argues that previous studies, by Bratton and Colleagues, on the role of elections in democracy were pessimistic. De Walle (2002) further argues that Africans have a certain universalism toward democracy.

Understanding the notion of democracy in Africa needs a thorough analysis of the events that transpired during the colonial era, for instance, after the independence and until the 1990s. But the objective in this essay is to cater a good grasp of democracy itself. Let us examine how the notion applies to Africa, although summarily here.

Assessing African Democracy

The term democracy is one of the most elusive ideas in political science. Bratton and De Walle (1994) note the term itself is commonly understood as one of the key ingredients of regime change. It could also be said that there is not a universal approach about what democracy entails, even in Western countries.

The literature is filled with contradictory theories about democracy (Lindberg, 2003; 2004). What is clear is that efforts to suppress democracy, or strategies to create a version of democracy that is not necessarily compatible with the democratization espoused by most European countries had a permanent impact on African polity.

Elections and Democracy

After the independence, most African countries held regular elections. Lindberg (2004) notes, "Africa had its first wave of democracy in the late 1950s" (p. 64). Even though elections were restricted, they were peaceful, fair, and free. Likewise, the outcomes of elections were seldom contested (Lindberg, 2004).

It is not debatable that the first African leaders after the independence were elected in competitive elections. Lindberg (2004) further notes, "This era of democratic elections, however, was to be short-lived" (p. 64). Elections were soon used as a tool to legitimize authoritarian regimes.

Most Western observers considered such regimes as despotic in nature. Patrimonial leaders headed those regimes (Bratton & De Walle, 1994). Before the 1990s, elections were not always the best tool to gauge the state of democracy in Africa. Election results did not accurately reflect the political reality of the African State itself.

Another reality is worth pointing out in the debate. It is irrefutable that elections in many African States were seldom free or fair (Bratton & De Walle, 1994). In similar instances, the military played a role in hampering democracy. A plethora of African States experienced coup d'états and other forms of political unrests.

Since the 1990s, I must admit, the likelihood for a better Africa consistently improved. Initiatives for democratic reforms across the continent had positive results. Although those efforts experienced some setbacks, at least since the end of the Cold War, there were significant improvements in the types of regimes that governed Africa. More often than not, democratic transitions had been smooth.

Despite those steps in the right direction, many African States are still struggling to find their path toward democracy. Authoritarian regimes are still the norm in many African States, although a handful of them. Until recently, Zimbabwe, which is a former British colony, was still ruled by an authoritarian regime.[4] Cameroon also had an authoritarian or a patrimonial leader. Thus, understanding the role of democracy and the nature of democratic institutions in Africa can be a daunting task.

Democracy and the Pre-Colonial Era

Is democracy an African feature? Perhaps this is not the case at all. To grasp the reason many African countries are still struggling to instill democratic principles, let us revisit the historical context in which democracy was implanted in the continent.

It is also important to understand the mechanism that led to creating democratic institutions. Granted, it might pose a challenge to understand the nature of Africa's drive toward democracy, mainly after the Cold War, without considering the role of Europeans in shaping the political identity of the continent. We must

---

[4] This is a reference to Robert Mugabe Regime, which held a grip in Zimbabwe for several decades.(Burke, 2017) Robert Mugabe held on to power for a long time. He died in 2019 at 95years of age. Learn more about his death here. (Cowell, 2019)

explore this role both before and after the independence.

African Democracy

Democracy is an imported feature of colonialism. Even so, the common belief is the nature of African democracy is a strange phenomenon. Democracy in Africa is different from other democracies around the world.

There is a truth to the preceding assertion. Bratton and De Walle (1994) notes that even among African countries, democracy does not apply evenly. Therefore, to understand democracy in Africa, one must ineluctably understand the role of colonialism on the continent.

African politicians often mimic ideals that were implanted by the colonial regimes. Put simply, the African State did not invent democracy on the continent. As Bratton and De Walle (1994) hint, one cannot remove the effect of neopatrimonialism on African politics.

An important feature of democracy is a peaceful regime transition (Lindberg, 2004). A democratic transition is, in and of itself, a process. In this case, a democratically elected government replaces another regime as the sovereign authority of the state. After a wave of independence, however, there were fewer democratic transitions on the African continent.

Bratton and De Walle (1997) contend that the democratic experiment in Africa was guided by the actions of political regimes. These actions, in turn, had been engrained in the political culture. They had been set up by many regimes overtime.

These political actions led to, what some may see as, pitting democratic institutions against each other. This reality led to a deeply entrenched institutional polarization in many African States. As a result, neopatrimonial practices are the core feature of African politics (Bratton & De Walle, 1994).

Approaches to Democracy in Africa

When it comes to democracy in Africa, Bratton and De Walle (1997) recognize the existence of several approaches. However, grasping the nature of African democracy remains a daunting task. Existing approaches underline the process (or the lack thereof) of democratizing the African State. They argue that democracy and regime changes can be best understood through the framework of a politico-institutional approach.

According to these scholars, seven approaches are often used to explain democracy in the African State. They include structural approach, contingent approach, international approach, domestic approach, economic approach, political approach, and politico-institutional approach. But these approaches tend to overlap.

In the structural approach, for instance, democracy is closely intertwined with politics. Politics guide social order. They guide expression in modern industrial society.

This relationship dictates how democracy evolves. From here, political changes must result from socioeconomic structures (Bratton & De Walle, 1997). In the contingent approach, they note that decisions and behaviors of individual political agents play a major role in democracy.

Notions about individual freedom guide choices in both the economy and politics. This approach also looks at the voting patterns of individuals. This method assumes that political outcomes are not pre-determined by the weight of structural precedent. Political initiatives incite political responses within society. In that sense, political events are interwoven with political actors.

Political outcomes are the results of interactions and bargaining. They provide a mere cleavage about democracy or a fantasy of that. Popular notions about the term democracy itself are based on the idea of compromise and concessions. This approach highlights the role of individual preferences. It underlines the role of political actors (Bratton & De Walle, 1997).

In the international approach, Bratton and De Walle (1997) argue that states and regimes do not function in a vacuum. They are part of an internal faction, which functions according to the directives of external cues or external entities. In this case, states influence regime activities and vice versa. Just the same, both states and regimes are influenced by international entities.

In essence, both state and regime actions are shaped by outside forces. From here, one could make the case that international forces play in important role on development initiatives. In the same vein, external forces influence political actors. They guide opposing political movements. In the domestic approach, regime transitions stem from, first, from the actors, the organizations, and the institutions that settles in the national arena (Bratton & De Walle, 1997, p. 31).

Bratton and De Walle (1997) note that African leaders resist outside influences. This resistance led to nationalist regimes, which clash with external interests. In the economic approach, these scholars argue that, although changes in material conditions mainly affect changes in politics, politics is always supreme. Politics and political actors play a prominent role in regime transitions.

The political approach centers on the role of the institutions that grant power. In post-colonial Africa, the major source of power comes from electoral institutions. Thus, political traditions played a major role in regime transitions. Nonetheless, those political traditions were seldom compatible with democratic ideals, notably in one-party systems (Bratton & De Walle, 1997).

In the politico-institutional approach, the interaction among political institutions is vital to understanding regime transition and democracy. Bratton and De Walle (1997) note that domestic politics play a significant role in regime transitions. Political struggles are often mediated through institutional settings, which favor some groups to the detriment of others.

Bratton and De Walle (1997) argue that the politico-institutional approach provides compelling explanations for understanding Africa's political liberalization during the 1990s. Macroeconomic and international factors, although important, they are also incomplete. A politico-institutional approach, for instance, highlights the neopatrimonialism in Africa.

Progress and Limits

Since the independence, there had been some progress in Africa. Many of these initiatives were limited. We must grasp the nature of the progress in Africa. It is also important to explore the limits of democratic reforms on the continent.

Colonial powers introduced democracy in Africa during the period of decolonization (Collier, 1982). All the way through the colonial era, elections were not always an issue. To be precise, before the independence, elections were regularly held in most African countries. But an important reality about African elections is also worth pointing out in the debate.

Elections seldom led to the political expression of the social order of modern industrial society. Often, introducing democratic institutions in the newly created African State was a strategy for preserving the status quo. Similar institutions were tailored to advance fundamental metropolitan interests (Collier, 1982, p. 30).

The Nature of Democracy in Africa

In 1848, in the French-controlled African regions, namely in Senegal, French citizens could take part in elections. Sometimes in the 1920s, other African colonies began experiencing limited franchise. For example, Kenya, Zambia (British) and Dahomey, Ivory Coast, Guinea, and Mali (French) were among the first countries to experience some form of elections.

The reality of elections did not set up a norm in various African States. Before 1945, for instance, few elections took place in Africa (Collier, 1982, p. 34). After the independence, most African colonies had experienced some form of universal suffrage or independent elections (Collier, 1982).

The French had a unique perceptive to elections in Africa. Colonial policy was made based on group assessments. Within the French controlled regions, it was conceivable that "Franchise was similar for all of the colonies" (Collier, 1982, p. 35).

The French had a two-college system. Each disposition was distinctly applied in West and Equatorial Africa. This approach was based on territorial assembly of each colony and indirect elections. The criteria to vote were based on individual identity and social status. This approach, it must also be noted, limited the number of seats until it was removed altogether.

Unlike the French, the British had a different approach to elections. British colonial policy about elections was unusual. It stressed on readiness for change. The British assessed ahead of time whether a colony was ready for change. The British set up colonial policies under the belief that a particular colony was ready for political changes. This approach created variant perspectives to democracy among the British colonies.

When it comes to democracy, however, the French were more successful in taming the regions they controlled, mostly in West Africa. There was a more gradual progression in that region. Many Africans ran for seats, though on a restricted franchise.

The understanding is that "experience with elections was substantially greater in French Africa than anywhere else in tropical Africa" (Collier, 1982, p. 45). The rate of introducing elections and mass participation had a particular effect on the colonies. These elections ushered in political, economical, and social changes.

The New Elite and Democracy

Because of changes in authority in Africa, the new ruling elites wanted control and domination over the recently settled political structures and institutions. This new era in African politics led to an array of conflicts (mostly political) about the ideological domination and the stewardship of the land. The new political elites sought to uphold the same democratic ideals that Europeans instilled on the African continent during colonial times.

Competitive elections threatened the status quo. Free elections affected the patterns of regime breakdown and the role of immediate post-independence electoral policy (Collier, 1982). Soon, the new elite realized that a Western democratic model, based on multi-party competitive suffrage, would not advance their objectives.

Multi-party and competitive elections became unsustainable. New leaders rapidly moved to abandon competitive party politics. As a result, there was a trend toward authoritarian regimes.

After the independence, electoral institutions were used as mechanisms to undermine democracy. Neopatrimonial leaders used electoral institutions as a means to assert presidential privileges (Bratton & De Walle, 1994). Electoral institutions that were supposed to instill democracy soon fell under the grip or the control of the new ruling class.

Privatizing the institutions, which symbolized a new era of democratization in Africa, worsened the problem of African democracy. Creating electoral institutions further undermined the democratization process. As Collier (1982) noted, "The introduction of democratic institutions, and particularly of universal suffrage, created a political resource for those indigenous elites who were in a position to take advantage of it" (p. 33).

After the independence, multi-party elections became an important issue, which the new elite had to address. Creating a one-party system became instrumental for new leaders. It was seen as the best way to control elections. A one-party system became the undeniable trademark of most authoritarian regimes in Africa.

Under authoritarian regimes, elections were often used as a *façade* for democracy (Collier, 1982). Those regimes used elections as a tool to strengthen their grip on power. Thereby, they legitimized their political reach; they reinforced their economic policies; they solidified their social agendas.

The Role of Elections in Regime Changes

Elections are always important, I would argue. They are good for keeping a healthy democracy. Elections may ease peaceful democratic transitions. In that sense, elections should have strengthened democratic values in Africa.

In true democracies, elections are supposed to be fair and free. They should promote real competitions. Ideally, in free elections, voters should not be subjected to pressure from external forces (Collier, 1982). Nevertheless, after the independence, elections had the opposite effect in many African States. Elections were not always free and fair.

Although the 1950s were marked by the transition from colonial authority to African leadership, it also marked the rise of one-party systems across the continent. Elections became the catalytic instrument that solidified many state-controlled activities. This period marked the death of true democracy in Africa.

Postcolonial elites set up authoritarian regimes in two ways. They did so through a one-party system and military coups. "Yet military leaders soon found it difficult to rule without recourse to civilian institutions" (Bratton & De Walle, 1994, p. 76). The electoral system was used to legitimize the one-party regime.

Most one-party regimes were different in the election they held and the degree of participation they allowed (Collier, 1982; Bratton & De Walle, 1994). In the former French colonies, for instance, elections were not competitive. They were similar to plebiscites.

In the former British colonies, on the other hand, elections were competitive. Those elections only included one-party competitions. Elections were used as a tool to reward, punish politicians, or to promote national interest issues. Those elections were also designed to produce popular support, which, in turn, contributed to providing legitimacy for the government (Collier, 1982, p. 135).

Since the 1950s until the end of the Cold War (that is, around 1990s), many African countries experienced an array of conflicts, which further threatened democracy. Bratton and Mattes (2001) argue, "Africa is a latecomer to democratization" (p. 107). For example, human rights issues, military coups, economic decadences, and environmental problems, to name a few, plagued many African States, arguably, to this day.

Collier (1982) notes that historical institutionalism played a significant role in democracy in Africa. What happened in the African continent after the independence was in part the result of setting up democratic ideals or democratic principles (Collier, 1982). In effect, one could not look at democratic efforts in Africa in positive lights, if one were to define democracy in either positive or negative ways (Collier, 1982). The experience was incompatible with the African reality.

Several other factors are also important to consider. Understanding democracy in Africa from a Western lens is a fruitless pursuit. It might be necessary to understand the role of regimes, regime changes, and patrimonial institutions.

The Decline of Neopatrimonialism

In the post-independence Africa, structural agency and institutionalism played a big role in democracy. Bratton and De Walle (1994) note that neopatrimonialism had a major impact on postcolonial Africa. Collier (1982) also notes that during that period, everything revolved around the leader.

Bratton and De Walle further point out that, "Authority is entirely personalized, shaped by the ruler's preferences rather than any codified system of laws" (Bratton & De Walle, 1994, p. 61). Those leaders favored the one-party system.

After the Cold War, there was a sense that Africa was changing directions. Several countries, including South Africa, Namibia, Cameroon, Zimbabwe, and Zaire, spearheaded a different approach toward democracy and governance. Those countries went from Africa's neopatrimonial norm to embrace a centralized form of government, which centered on strong legal-administrative procedures (Bratton & De Walle, 1994).

The Need for Progress

In the early 1990s, Sub-Saharan Africa underwent great political changes (De Walle, 2002). After the Cold War, many African countries experienced a democratic revival. Bratton and Mattes (2001) note, "Africans (so defined) overwhelmingly support democracy and reject authoritarian regimes" (p. 108).

Africans aspire to political freedom (Bratton & Mattes, 2001). The neopatrimonial approach to governance became untenable. Bratton and De Walle (1994) note that it was obvious for many countries that neopatrimonial practices caused chronic issues, which also hampered economic growth.

Neopatrimonial practices had other effects. They hindered ethnic plurality. Neopatrimonial leaders could no longer legitimate their rule. Before the prospects of social unrests, the foundation of many authoritarian regimes began to crumble (Bratton & De Walle, 1994). Authoritarian rulers could no longer control regime transitions.

A slew of political and economic crises created the possibility for regime transitions to come from society, rather than elite power (Bratton & De Walle, 1994, p. 83). After the Cold War, however, there were noticeable improvements toward true democracy in many African States. There were improvements in political freedom. Political liberalization led to opening societies, which, in turn, had positive impacts on citizen rights.

After the Cold War as well, there was a partial opening of non-democratic regimes. Most African regimes favored human rights and political freedom, which included the right to vote. In South Africa, for example, there were noticeable efforts toward legalizing political parties. The ANC, which had been previously classified as a terrorist group, was legalized. In that country, political prisoners were released.

During that time, Nelson Mandela, a prominent politician figure, was released from prison after many years in captivity. There were also improvements in other respects in many African societies. For example, there were fewer limits on access to information. As a result, the media enjoyed more freedom.

Between 1989 and 2000, there were approximately seventy presidential elections in sub-Saharan Africa. Those elections spread across 48 countries and involved more than one candidate. In essence, "The vast majority of African States are now multiparty electoral regimes" (De Walle, 2002, p. 67). That being noted, not all these improvements were without limits.

Assessing Limits

Democracy is elusive (Lindberg, 2003), especially when one group (or a single party) held a grip on power for many years. Various terms are often used to depict democracy in the African State. The term "A failed state" is, by far, one of the popular ways of depicting African countries.

The use of disparaging terms is often the result of mistaken assumptions about the African State itself and perhaps its political culture. Ill-advised observers often attach inaccurate meanings to the term democracy in Africa. African countries are regarded as undemocratic, even if the structural underpinnings of democracy or democratic ideals in the region come from external forces, namely western powers.

It is worthy of acknowledgment that the road toward democracy on the African continent was difficult for many countries. As argued throughout this essay, democracy is not endogenous to Africa. Rather, it is a foreign ideal. It is undeniable that the effects of colonial institutions are still present in many ways in African polity.

Anti-democratic traditions were not wiped out (De Walle, 2002). Although most countries are democratic, some states still have, what De Walle (2002) referred to as, "Hybrid regimes." Those hybrid regimes thrive in states that are between a full-fledged democracy and electoral autocracy.

In other states, power still lies in the hands of the president and a small ruling circle. "Such neopatrimonial rule is inherently antidemocratic because it is based on the private appropriation of public goods" (De Walle, 2002, p. 69). I would concede that there were many actions toward a democratic path in Africa.

It must nonetheless be echoed that ideals about power grabbing and coup d'états are still valued in most African political circles. Bratton and De Walle (1997) note that the faces of antidemocratic initiatives only changed on the surface. On the other hand, the ideal of the African State remained the same.

Democratic Consolidation in Africa

When it comes to the African continent, the notion of democracy may apply in many ways. Bratton and De Walle (1997) note that ambiguities about democracy are the result of the various approaches to democracy in Africa. There is an "Array of competing explanations about regime change" (Bratton & De Walle, 1997, p. 19).

While admitting the utility of the different approaches about the reason democracies are installed and consolidated, these scholars admit the impetus of those divergent views in promoting a better understanding of African democracy. Democratization is never an easy process. Africa's experimentation with this concept was not futile though. Many states are now on the verge of perfecting their approach to democracy.

Since the independence, Africa has experienced various types of regimes. None of them was democratic. In single-party regimes, there were no real competitions. You could join the party. But you could not contest the results.

Many states liberalized the political system. But they never intended to embrace democracy. There were changes in the electoral system. Still, the dominant party never lost.

There was also a partial opening of authoritarian systems. This approach was short of allowing the party to choose governmental leaders. Most often, these initiatives had been in futility. After the Cold War, however, there was a genuine push toward true democratic transitions and political reforms, as noted in South Africa.

Defining the Term Democracy

What does the term democratic consolidation mean? The notion commonly known as *Democratic consolidation* could be understood as the process by which a regime is strengthened so it becomes relatively immune to breakdown. The idea is that all political actors accept democracy as the only game in town. Since the independence, many African States went from authoritarian rule to liberalization and transition.

After the Cold War, many African countries raced toward democratic consolidation. This trend has not really changed. Current political actors recognized democracy as the only game in town. For that reason, I am optimistic about the prospect of democracy in Africa.

I must also point out that my views about the prospects of democracy are based on the many improvements the continent witnessed within the last few years. There is perhaps a model shift in the way democratic institutions are influenced by political actors. It would not be farfetched to argue that individuals [politicians], as opposed to a regime apparatus, play a more prominent role in democratic efforts.

In most African countries, there is a sense that democracy is important for economic progress. Within the context of globalization, democracy is considered supreme. On the surface, many African leaders understand the irrefutable implications [or the ramifications] of espousing undemocratic avenues.

Many states give the impression that they would uphold democratic rules. Political actors also agree that free and fair elections are the only means of power. Therefore, there is hope for democratic consolidation in Africa.

The Fading Colonialism in Africa

Around the 1950s, there was a broken, if not a visible, withdrawal of direct colonial authority. That discontinuity led to dramatic changes in Africa. Those changes, in turn, led to the introduction of electoral institutions. These institutions did not benefit democracy as a whole.

At first, electoral institutions carried the trademarks of a Western democratic model, which favored a multi-party system. The problem is that "Soon after independence, it became clear that the Western democratic model, based on multi-party competitive elections, would not be followed in Africa" (Collier, 1982, p. 95). The African States became synonymous of political instability, economic deprivation, and a symbol of undemocratic governance.

The same institutions that were supposed to instill democracy led to the rise of several one-party regimes and military governments. Competitive elections were later canceled. Often, authoritarian regimes dominated the land through one-party or military regimes. Nevertheless, elections continued to be a part of most African States, except for some military regimes, whom had a tendency to suspend elections altogether.

After the Cold War, there was a new trend. Most states rejected authoritarian rule. The new tendency in African democracy is toward upholding the rule of law.

There is an interesting pattern in African democracy. After World War II, tropical Africa witnessed changing forms of political supremacy (Collier, 1982). That period of democratic instability lasted through the end of the Cold War.

Since the 1990s, many African States espoused a different approach toward democracy. I am confident that Africa will be able to consolidate its current democratic reforms. Thus, it would not be fanciful to say that the continent is on the right path. I have enough reasons to be optimistic for Africa.

PART 4

Essay Three: The Ruling Elite

CHAPTER 5

Groomed to Rule Africa

IT IS UNDENIABLE that Africa today is different from what it used to be. But to grasp the political reality of the continent, we must delve deeper in its past. As outlined here thus far, that past is the result of a deeply flawed colonial experiment.

After the colonial experience, the African State that existed before colonialism existed no more. Colonialism reordered the continent's political landscape (Young, 1994). These adjustments had a marked effect on the institutions that colonial powers themselves created. They also affected the social structures that these powers settled. Such structures were designed specifically to be used or to be ruled by the elite, which the colonial powers groomed specifically for that task.

Africa's problems are best understood through a domestic lens. The notion of power politics is a major subject of debate in postcolonial Africa. Political regimes, patrimonial leaders, and other social structures had a significant influence in conflicts. Collier and Gunning (1999) note that certain conditions, namely geographic and demographic, predisposed Africa's path.

Crawford Young echoes a similar view. He argues that after the independence, African leaders inherited the Africa that was given to them by Europeans (Young, 1994). In the same vein, Collier and Gunning (1999) argue that colonial heritage hindered Africa's growth.

How did colonialism negatively affect the African State? According to Collier and Gunning (1999), "the most popular argument is that for much of the post-colonial period most African governments were undemocratic" (p. 10). Crawford Young similarly argues that perspective. Young traces this tendency since creating the African State.

Although each regime or each ruler had its own aura or his own identity, the effects of their actions were similar. The state, nevertheless, was structured to simplify certain political or ideological inclinations, regardless of the regime in place. Young (1994) notes an important difference between state, regime, and ruler. When we speak of state, the general idea that usually comes to mind is the notion of permanent entities, which also presumes perennity (Young, 1994, p. 40).

Regime and ruler, Young notes, are less stable. They hold their own mechanism for reproduction (Young, 1994, p. 40). While a regime could change, the state would keep its structures. Nevertheless, states had to hold a few fundamental features.

From Young's perspective, the African State lacked most of the important features of a true state. Therefore, Young questions the existence of the African State, not only during the colonial era, but also during postcolonial times. Young assesses several needs for a state to exist. He hints that the African State, both during and after colonial times, failed to meet those criteria.

Examining Colonial Structures

The colonial structures in the African State had been inculcated overtime. The effects of those structures soon became obvious. For example, immediately after the independence, there was a vague of optimism in Africa. There was also a positive upbeat for the continent in various parts of the world.

The common belief was that Africa should do away with the old. This was the best way—some observers were convinced—for the African State itself to embrace a sustainable path toward progress. Nevertheless, there were warning signs, which suggested that things would not be that easy for Africa.

Young notes, "Rene Dumont warned in 1962 that African was off to a poor start" (Young, 1994, p. 3). At the time, the issues that the African State faced were mostly structural. Even so, there were other factors, which appeared conducive to instability and underdevelopment.

Soon after the independence, it became clear for the elite that democracy would not benefit their interests. They also used the state to create new mechanisms that would allow them to remain in power.

The African State saw the rise of one-party systems. Soon, there were rebellions. There were civil wars. Autocratic governments began to take hold within the continent.

Young notes that the African State had a rough start. Although there was ample optimism for Africa after the independence, positive expectations rapidly evaporated. Before the meager performance of the new leaders, confidence in the state became low. Many states became synonymous of failure.

While some states progressed, others failed miserably. True, Botswana and Mauritius stood out as positive examples of progress. Other states, including Sudan, Somalia, Zaire, and Mozambique deserve a separate category, markedly when it comes to the nature of the disarray and the decay that characterize these States (Young, 1994, p. 2). Ghana also stood out as a symbol of failure. By the 1980s, there was a growing sense of pessimism. It seemed as though most African States had failed.

Overtime, the optimism in Africa began to fade away, as frustrations and disillusions mounted. People no longer trusted their leaders. Some observers questioned the relevancy of the state. The delinquency of the state created a vacuum of authority. The African State was weak.

There were little efforts by the new leaders to serve the population. According to Young (1994), these antecedents are not surprising, considering that the African State did not grow organically. The African State itself was not formed organically. It did not come out of African societies.

The African State was the product of the Colonial State. The state was designed by the colonial regime to serve the interests of foreign actors. The African State was both overdeveloped and soft. Therefore, the State itself was erected artificially on the foundations of the Colonial State (Young, 1994, p. 60).

The African State did not hold the administrative and political means to make a real difference. The state lacked the capacity to govern itself. As previously argued, this was not by coincidence.

A Legitimate State

Crawford Young questions whether the African State should be considered as a legitimate state. The author looks at the state from a theoretical and historical standpoint. He notes that states nourish the want to amass and preserve power through their institutions (Young, 1994, p. 21).

States also play a role in the international system. Limits, such as politics or political systems, including bureaucratic politics, could lead to institutional fragmentation. That new arrangement of the recently created African State hampered their capacity to exert power.

This reality is in part the result of structural fragmentation and divergence among actors. The presumption is that human agency played a role in constraining the capacity of the state to exert power. This is perhaps what happened to the African State. The colonial regime created the elite, which, arguably, had its own agendas.

Another limit is a detachment between state actors and the population at large. The political elite had a different approach to Africa's development than the people did. Within that perspective, questioning the legitimacy of the state could indisputably lead to conflicts.

In defining the features of the state, Crawford Young notes that a state must have eight crucial characteristics, which includes territory, sovereignty, population, power, law, the state as a nation, the state as an international actor, and the state as an idea. Young believes that the African State fell short in some of these important traits.

Young argues that a state must have a territory. This is "the most fundamental trait" (Young, 1994, p. 26). A state must have a population. He stresses on the notion of civil society. Rule is exercised over an ensemble of human subject residents within a territorial jurisdiction. A state must be sovereign.

The idea of sovereignty vests a final and absolute authority (Young, 1994, p. 27). A state must exert power (Young, 1994). This is its natural capacity to secure habitual obedience and defense through legitimacy, custom, or fear (Young, 1994, p. 31).

Law is an important feature of the state. A state picks up its legal status as a legal domain through laws. Thus, a state must strive to uphold the notion of nationalism.

The state is also an international actor. A state must aim for external sovereignty to preserve its survival. The state must exist as an idea, which includes affective orientations, images, and expectations imprinted in the mind of its subjects (Young, 1994, p. 33).

A state plays a historical role. A state has certain imperatives that guide its actions. A state must seek to impose supremacy by engaging in struggles to ensure supremacy of their authority (Young, 1994, p. 35).

Autonomy is an important need for a state as well. A state must assert its autonomy both internally and externally. A state must preserve its security (that is, national security) and instilling public safety within the territory it governs.

A state must seek legitimacy through its institutions. It must seek habitual compliance in the consent to its rule. A state must strengthen the ability of rulers to elaborate institutions. It must increase collective goods provided by the state. States need revenue. It must extract resources necessary for performing its other roles (Young, 1994, p. 38).

Amassing Wealth

Aiming for wealth was also a function of the state. The newly created Africans States sought to amass wealth through a capitalist development. Crawford Young notes that the Colonial State does not meet the needs of a state per se, at least as previously outlined, for the Colonial State lacked three crucial elements.

In this case, the Colonial State was lacking of the notion of nationhood. It lacked any ideal about the important of self-determination. The newly created African State existed under the fancies of former rulers. The new state depended on the organizational apparatus and the institutional structures, which had been put in place by the former colonial regime.

The newly created state had to make its own dent in international polity. According to Young, the Colonial State "was not an actor in the international scene; it was occasionally a stage hand" (Young, 1994, p. 43). The author further argues that the notion of a state could not apply to colonial Africa (Young, 1994).

One reason the newly created African State could not be viewed as a state in the true sense of the term because it was produced out of the *Bula Matari*. This bone-crushing strategy was carried out all over the continent. When the Europeans arrived in Africa, they perfected colonization to a degree where they set up the notion of stateness within the structures of the Colonial State.

The Europeans could infiltrate civil society. That infiltration later became the basis on which post-colonial African was founded. Young notes that "African societies were to encounter a colonial master equipped with doctrines of domination and capabilities for the exercise of rule that went far beyond those available in earlier times and other places" (Young, 1994, p. 77).

From this historical perspective, Young argues that the African State was destined to fail. The structures of African society were pre-determined by the Colonial State, which, by design, had omitted certain features. Such traits were quintessential for the existence of a free and independent state.

The African State came about because European countries were in a search for power. The French, the British, the Portuguese, the Belgians, the Germans, and the Italians sought out to pick up as much land as possible. Young (1994) notes, "from 1875 to 1900, in an extraordinary moment of imperial enthusiasm, a veritable collective intoxication of colonial expansion, set in" (Young, 1994, p. 83).

Further, the author points out that Africans were embroiled in a "complex web of political, economic, and ideological factors" (Young, 1994, p. 83). Those factors later became the basis of the African State in postcolonial Africa. As a result, new African leaders had little to no chance of achieving success.

Setting up the African State

The African State was set up in two phases. During the first phase, the continent witnessed, "a brief phase of actual conquest" (Young, 1994, p. 90). During that stage, there were endless skirmishes, which were related to frontier over white land claims. This period marked "colonial partition and the implementation of doctrines championing the 'imperialism of free trade' and low-cost informal empire, through coastally-based zones of mercantile influence" (Young, 1994, p. 82).

The second phase was marked by the actual state construction and the irrefutable imposition of institutionalized rule. This period set up a moment when the African community started to recognize colonial authority. During this stage, new political kingdoms were erected; they later led to constant subjecting of the African population (Young, 1994, p. 95).

Colonial forces settled dominance all around the continent. They used local security forces, including tribe leaders. They also used laws as a tool to enforce their supremacy.

It is worth noting that during this time, the Europeans piled up an extensive amount of wealth. Young (1994) further notes, "all fiscal traits led to the African subject" (Young, 1994, p. 126). Then, the African economy was based on rural activities. Europeans used local tribes and chiefs to collect taxes (Young, 1994, p. 128).

Assessing Viewpoints

While I do not agree with Crawford Young's approach on certain issues related to Africa's political reality, which many African leaders faced during the postcolonial era, I share many of the views he echoed about the construction of the African State itself. The assessment that Young outlines in the previous section of the manuscript is illustrative of how European forces shaped the African continent itself. It is also indicative of how they set up the structures that new African leaders would later follow. That is why I share Young's assessment of the origins of the continent's problems.

Other scholars converge in the same direction. By referencing Crawford Young and his beliefs about the African State, one could make the argument that the foundation of the African State itself was the product of colonialism. But the colonialism, on its own, was not perfect, at least if we were to examine that experience from the theoretical perspective. We would not come up with a similar conclusion if we were to examine the creation of the African State by referencing popular understandings about the idea of a state or if we were to settle on what a state should be.

The notion of state that the Europeans set up in Africa was skewed to serve their own interests. Even though new leaders had replaced European dominion, certain characteristics of the state were conducive to their failure. While "the state was no longer the custodian of liberation and development, but the instrument of extractor and exploitation" still prevailed (Young, 1994, p. 4). For the same reasons, new leaders could adjust the rules to favor both their interests and foreign interests.

The transition from colonial control became the trademark of political and economic tragedies on the African continent. Post-colonial Africa was plagued with all sorts of ills and social problems, including political discordance, bad governance, competition for resources, and corruption. These problems weaken the state. They also led to conflicts. Herbst (2000) notes, rebels "face states that are exceptionally weak and which may be in a process of advanced disintegration" (p. 283).

Most observers believe that the problems that crippled progress or important initiatives, which would make it possible for the African State to develop itself, were the results of poor leadership. Practices such as patrimonialism and corruption hindered development. Moreover, such practices stalled economic progress, some believe. They eventually increased political conflicts between the different elite groups that sought to consolidate and preserve their grip on power and their dominion on African polity. These practices, some might also say, had a negative effect on regime outcomes. They finally led to the eventual destruction of the state.

Young (1994) argues that structures played in important role in creating the African State. Although colonial forces set up different strategies to compel African polity and to conquer Africa, the result was similar across the board. For example, Europeans used settlers, charter companies, military forces, treaties, and missionaries to conquer Africans. They also used direct and indirect rules to infiltrate traditional African rules.

Europeans introduced new forms of social exclusions. Some Europeans used different sets of legal codes to distinguish the treatments Africans were entitled to, as opposed to whites.

But this did not occur only during the colonial era.

These realities were also reproduced during the postcolonial era in Africa. New leaders sought to strengthen their grip on power by setting up undemocratic regimes. Those regimes tented to exclude political groups, namely ethnic groups. They created institutions that favored their political brand. Bratton and De Walle (1997) note the use of political institutions to drive and control elections in many African States.

Collier (1982) further notes that, although colonial powers introduced democracy on the African continent during the period of decolonization, in postcolonial Africa, electoral institutions seldom led to the political expression of social order. The introduction of democratic institutions was tailored to advance fundamental metropolitan interests (Collier, 1982, p. 30).

New leaders further developed European strategies to get revenue. They imposed taxes. It was a *Head tax*. They exploited natural resources, including minerals. While new leaders did not instrument forced labor (slave labor), they created a climate where Africans were forced to work in urban places for minuscule a pay.

Just laws were passed to make it illegal to be unemployed under the colonial regime, under postcolonial governmental setups, new leaders set up policies that were damaging to the state as a whole. Such policies benefited fractions within the African society. Throughout Africa, for example, there was a search to destroy agriculture and to replace it by an industrial labor force. That industrial force favored the elites and their friends.

Just as in the past, Africans were pressured into working next to nothing. It was the continuity of the capitalistic economy, which had been set up by Europeans in the 1800s. Nothing had changed in Africa, really.

Just as before (that is, in colonial Africa) in postcolonial Africa, external trade policies and practices eased the rapid build-up of foreign currency and wealth. New African leaders set up monetary policies that eventually destroyed the state economy. The African State switched from a chiefly rural or agricultural economy to a more industrial economy.

The best land was taken to produce things that are exported (Bates, 1981). Therefore, the population starved; food had to be imported

(Bates, 1981). There was a shift from local economy to global economy.

People no longer produced; they imported most of their food (Bates, 1981). This reality increased Africa's dependency on foreign entities. That also made it possible for foreign agencies to take hold on the newly created African State.

Commonalities in Viewpoints

No doubt, the Africans States strived to gain dominance, security, build-up, and legitimacy. After the Cold War, many African States saw a change from military to civilian rule. States tried to increase attention and popular interests by building schools, roads, and infrastructures. As Young (1994) argues, states were more successful at setting up power.

The African State failed to settle legitimacy, revenue, infrastructure, and building-up wealth. But they were only good at the sheer exercise of power. This was in part because of the remnants of the Bula Matari, which is the legacy of the colonial period. The new African leaders used the same tactics to oppress political opponents.

Crawford Young did not exaggerate in his assessment of the African State. The Colonial State guided and helped frame the postcolonial era in Africa, both institutionally and structurally. Young accurately encapsulates the African problem.

Not everyone agrees with Young's assessment of the African reality though. Even Young himself recognizes that the search for understanding Africa's problems resulted in several explanations, including natural calamities, population growth, AIDS, international trade relations, and political calamities (Young, 1994, p. 8). Thus, Africa remains an ever-lasting puzzle.

To reiterate, I share the views Crawford Young echoes about the role of foreign agencies on the continent. It is irrefutable that colonialism played a prominent role in the failure of Africa. Thus, agency contributed to efforts designed specifically to collapse the African State.

Young (1994) further states that historic determinants, in this case, "modeled the contemporary state and shaped it behavioral imperatives" (Young, 1994, p. 9). The Colonial State "totally reordered political space, societal hierarchies and cleavages, and modes of economic production" (Young, 1994, p. 9). Based on the previous assessments, it would be shortsighted to blame Africans solely for the continent's troubles, mostly after the independence.

PART 5

Closing Thoughts

CHAPTER 6

Hope for Africa

IS THERE ANY HOPE for Africa? I would say yes. In saying that, I recognize there are striking problems on the continent.

In contrast with some of the views echoed here thus far, it is obvious that there is a reality on the African continent. Environmental issues, chiefly climate changes and infectious diseases, continually play a prominent role in hampering progress in Africa. Does that mean there is no hope for the continent? I would not say that.

One way to look at the previous question is by relying on the recent developments in Africa, which, for a better or worse, captivated the world's attention. For example, terrorism is rampant in various parts of the continent, chiefly in Nigeria.(BBC News, 2016) Natural disasters continue to affect Africa as a whole. The continent experienced some of the worst health crisis in recent memory.

The sequels of the *Ebola Outbreak* had a marked effect in various regions.(Center for Disease Control and Prevention, 2020) Nonetheless, we must assess the future of Africa from a more positive outlook. We must look at the continent from the lens of history and not from a post-Ebola mindset. The hope is that Ebola or any other types of infectious diseases could be contained.

While the prospects can be uncertain for Africa, not every piece of news from that part of the world is bad. When it comes to Ebola, the prognostics are favorable (Ohlheiser, 2015). There is a lot going on in various parts of the continent. From here, we could examine Africa by exploring its signs of progress. There is no need to linger on the many issues that the continent, as a whole of course, abstained from over the last few years.

Stability in Africa

Africa is more stable than ever before. In recent years, the continent made progress, both on the political end and on the economic front. A recent survey by the Legatum Institute found that several African countries are among the most prosperous nation in that part of the world.[5]

South Africa and Nigeria are among the biggest economies in the region (Edozien, 2015). Over the years, these countries made notable leaps to become self-sustainable. A few African countries are among the most prosperous nations in the continent. Others are even competing at a global level. Put differently, the prospects are not that grim for the African continent.

---

[5]Legatum Institute, "2014 Africa Prosperity Report," *Legatum Institute* (blog), December 11, 2014, https://li.com/reports/2014-africa-prosperity-report/.

 ; (Brien, 2020)

It is undeniable that Africa has been making significant strides. While the recent Ebola outburst hampered positive trends toward progress, the continent is still advancing in the right direction. There are enough reasons to be optimistic for the continent's future.

Africa, some might say, has a new face now. Most African countries are moving in the right direction, at the right pace, and at the right time. The conjuncture has never been that bright for the continent as a whole. Put differently, it would not be farfetched to say that Africa is doing all right. But that does not negate the fact that the continent is still facing tremendous challenges.

I agree that there are important problems in Africa. That, in and of itself, is not a novel reality. From a historical lens, achieving progress in Africa has always been a constant struggle. However, that does not mean that Africa is condemned to struggle.

By relying on the previous assessments, we could make the argument that, as opposed to the postcolonial era, Africa has a better foundation to succeed in a world dominated by its former masters. Thus, the continent has a much greater chance for continued success. Many African countries are well poised to uplift themselves. For these reasons, I would contend that there is hope for Africa.

What about you, do you see a prosperous Africa in a near future? I hope the answer is yes. If not, let us agree to disagree then.

CHAPTER 7

Important Questions

WE HAVE DISCUSSED several important issues in this short compilation. As we wind down the manuscript, let us revisit a few facets of the arguments echoed in the text. Let us revisit a few questions posed throughout the document. The following includes a list of important questions, which address the argumentations we debated in the book.[6]

Question 1

What is most striking about Mahmood Mamdani's depiction of the African State?

Answer

One of the most sticking approaches about Mahmood Mamdani's depiction of the African State is there never existed a single African State. Contrary to previous viewpoints, Mamdani's perspective stands out as a stunning departure from the common beliefs about Africa. This author's writings suggest a change of model in African studies.

Mamdani claims that both Africans and Europeans are to blame for the African State struggled to find its way. Just as Crawford Young or Jeffrey Herbst, Mamdani further notes that through trial and error, the Europeans were

---

[6] Note: These questions are based on several class assignments (Villanova University/fall 2013).

able to instill their dominance on the African State.

Mamdani notes that certain structures that had been put in place by the Europeans lasted long after the independence. Those structures, he argues, created disunity and division. This reality in turn led to policies and political frameworks that further weakened the African State.

Mamdani suggests that there were two African States within the African State: a state that was governed by formal rules (as he put it, direct rules) and a state that was governed by informal rules or indirect rules. The indirectly ruled state was relegated to the fancies of tribes through the means of institutional policies and practices.

Mamdani refutes the notion that South Africa was exceptional. The author further argues that the South African experiment was adjusted. It was refined over time. The true origin of Apartheid, Mamdani notes, was based on a "divide and conquer" strategy. Both Great Britain and France had perfected this approach.

Question 2

What does Mamdani mean by the terms "bifurcated state" and "institutional segregation"?

Answer

The term "bifurcated state" sketches two form of power under a single ruling authority. The term also sketches a dual approach to colonization the European used over an indigenous majority in Africa. Mamdani notes that the African bifurcated state was comprised of two forms of rules: a direct and an indirect ruling system.

In the direct ruling system, there was a single legal order. Europeans devised the early response as a means to address administrative issues in Africa (that is, the problem of managing the colonies). This approach was used as a form of urban civil power.

In the indirect ruling system, proxies, such as tribes and chiefs, exerted power on the population. Those proxies were accountable only to the Europeans. This control suggested a form of rural or tribal authority. Indirect rule sketches the mode of domination the Europeans espoused over the peasantry.

The term "institutional segregation" referred to a form of segregation by institutions. Institutions were used as the primary means to separate between the natives and European settlers. This approach was grounded in a politically enforced organization of ethnic pluralism. Within the context of the native question or problem, native institutions were heavily influenced by European norms, even though natives were territorially separated from white settlers.

Question 3

How does institutional segregation differ from territorial segregation?

Answer

In institutional segregation, the natives were not forced to assimilate into a common type. This approach comprised policies of institutional homogenization. It was a broader form of racial segregation.

This approach was a way of preserving native institutions. It was also a way of meeting the labor demands of a growing economy. Territorial segregation, on the other hand, was based on the territorial separation between the natives and European settlers. This was done through ethnic disparities and cultural differences.

Question 4

What does Mamdani mean by "customary law"?

Answer

Customary law could be understood as the laws of the tribes. This understanding was not in singular. Carrying out such laws principally sought to promote social equilibrium. It was an administratively driven affair within the African State.

This was a law, which sought to regulate nonmarket relations in land, in personal (family), and in community affairs. Still, there was not a single customary law that governed all the tribes. These laws varied, depending on the characteristics of the tribes.

Question 5

How did civic authority differ from customary authority in colonial Africa?

Answer

The difference between civic authority and customary authority was race and tribes. While civic authority was most guided by racial beliefs, a tribal lens guided customary authority. Civic authority was the sources of civil law, which, in turn, framed civil rights in civil society. The former (that is, civil authority) was more practical than analytical. The latter (colonial authority) was more ideological than historical.

Question 6

How was African colonial authority transformed by the colonial experience?

Answer

The African colonial authority was transformed by the colonial reality. That experience led to two constellations of power in the postcolonial

Africa. The colonial experience created the following political frameworks: conservative and radical.

In the conservative spectrum, the hierarchy of the local state apparatus, that is, from chiefs to headmen, continued unaltered after independence. From a more radical spectrum, there were some noticeable changes. They set up a uniform customary law. This law was applicable to all peasants, regardless of ethnicity or ethnic affiliations. Nevertheless, versions of the bifurcated state remained in place long after the colonial era.

References

BBC News. (2016, November 24). Who are Boko
    Haram? *BBC News*.
    https://www.bbc.com/news/world-africa-
    13809501

Brien, S. (2020, February 3). The Africa
    Prosperity Report 2019-2020. *Legatum
    Institute*. https://li.com/reports/the-africa-
    prosperity-report-2019-2020/

Burke, J. (2017, November 15). Robert Mugabe's
    grip on Zimbabwe ebbing away after military
    takes control. *The Guardian*.
    https://www.theguardian.com/world/2017/no

v/15/mugabe-family-military-takes-control-
zimbabwe-mnangagwa

Center for Disease Control and Prevention.
(2020, March 17). *2014-2016 Ebola Outbreak in
West Africa | History | Ebola (Ebola Virus
Disease) | CDC.*
https://www.cdc.gov/vhf/ebola/history/2014-
2016-outbreak/index.html

Collier, P., & Gunning, J. W. (1999). Why Has
Africa Grown Slowly? *Journal of Economic
Perspectives, 13,* 3–22.

Collier, P., Sambanis, N., & Bigombe, B. (2000).
Policies for Building Post-Conflict Peace.
Journal of African Economies, 9(3), 323.

Cowell, A. (2019, September 6). Robert Mugabe,
Strongman Who Cried, 'Zimbabwe Is Mine,'
Dies at 95. *The New York Times.*
https://www.nytimes.com/2019/09/06/obituar
ies/robert-mugabe-dead.html

Edozien, F. (2015, January 12). *The key difference
between Africa's two biggest economies right
now.* Quartz. https://qz.com/324739/the-key-
difference-between-africas-two-biggest-
economies-right-now/

Graybill, L. S. (2004). Pardon, Punishment, and
Amnesia: Three African Post-Conflict

Methods. *Third World Quarterly*, 25(6), 1117–1130.

Legatum Institute. (2014, December 11). 2014 Africa Prosperity Report. *Legatum Institute*. https://li.com/reports/2014-africa-prosperity-report/

Ohlheiser, A. (2015, March 23). *Ebola outbreak could be 'gone by the summer,' United Nations says*. Washington Post. https://www.washingtonpost.com/news/morning-mix/wp/2015/03/23/a-year-ago-an-ebola-outbreak-was-declared-it-could-be-gone-by-the-summer-un-says/.

Essay 1

Chazan, N., Lewis, P., Mortimer, R., Rothchild, D., Stedman, S. J. (1999). *Politics and society in contemporary Africa.* Boulder, London: Lynne Rienner Publishers.

Englebert, P. (2000). *State legitimacy and development in Africa.* Boulder, London: Lynne Rienner Publishers.

Herbst, J. (2000). States and power in Africa: Comparative lessons in authority and control. Princeton, NJ: Princeton University Press.

Mamdani, M. (1996). Citizen and subject: Contemporary Africa and the legacy of late colonialism. Princeton, NJ: Princeton University Press.

Tordoff, W. (2002). *Government and politics in Africa.* Bloomington, Indiana: Indiana University Press.

Young, C. (1994). *The African Colonial State in comparative perspective.* New Haven, CT: Yale University Press.

Essay 2

Bratton, M., De Walle, N. V. (1994). "Neo-patrimonial rule in Africa," in Michael & Nicolas Van De Walle (eds.), Democratic Experiments in Africa: Regime transitions in comparative perspective. 61-82.

Bratton, M., De Walle, N. V. (1997). *Democratic experiments in Africa.* New York & Cambridge: Cambridge University Press. Chapter 1, "Approaches to Democratization," 19-48.

Bratton, M., Mattes, R. (2001). How people view democracy: Africans' surprising universalism. *Journal of democracy, 12(*1): 107-121. The Johns Hopkins University Press. *DOI: 10.1353/jod.2001.0002.*

Collier, R. B. (1982). Regimes in tropical Africa: Changing forms of supremacy, 1945-1975. Berkeley: University of California Press.

De Walle, N. V. (2002). Africa's range of regimes: 1957. *Journal of Democracy, 13(*2): 66-80. The Johns Hopkins University Press. *DOI: 10.1353/jod.2002.0032.*

Lindberg, L. S. (2003), It's our time to "Chop": Do elections in Africa feed neo- patrimonialism rather than counter-act it?, *Democratization, 10(*2): 121-140. DOI:10.1080/714000118. Retrieved from: http://dx.doi.org/10.1080/714000118

Lindberg, L. S. (2004). The democratic qualities of competitive elections: Participation, competition and legitimacy in Africa. *Commonwealth & Comparative Politics, 42(*1): 61-105. DOI: 10.1080/14662040408565569: http://dx.doi.org/10.1080/14662040408565569

Essay 3

Bates, R. H. (1981). Markets and states in tropical Africa: The political basis of agricultural policies. London, England: University of California Press.

Bratton, M., De Walle, N. V. (1997). *Democratic experiments in Africa.* New York & Cambridge: Cambridge University Press. Chapter 1, "Approaches to Democratization," 19-48.

Collier, R. B. (1982). Regimes in tropical Africa: Changing forms of supremacy, 1945-1975. Berkeley: University of California Press.

Collier, P. Gunning, J. T. (1999). Why Africa grown slowly? *The Journal of Economic Perspectives. 13(3).* 3-22.

Herbst, J. (2000). States and power in Africa: Comparative lessons in authority and control. Princeton, NJ: Princeton University Press.

Young, C. (1994). *The African Colonial State in comparative perspective.* New Haven, CT: Yale University Press.

PART 6

Miscellaneous

Index

About the Author

BEN WOOD JOHNSON, Ph.D.
Dr. Johnson is a social observer. He is also a multidisciplinary scholar. He writes about Philosophy, Legal Theory, and Foreign Policy. He also writes about Education (School Leadership), Politics, Ethics, Race, and Crime.

Dr. Johnson is a Penn State graduate. He holds a Doctorate in Educational Administration/Leadership, a Master's degree in Political Science, a Master's degree in Public Administration, and a Bachelor's degree in Criminal Justice.

Dr. Johnson worked in law enforcement. He attended John Jay College of Criminal Justice. He is fluent in many languages, including, but not limited to, English, French, Spanish, Portuguese, and Italian.

Dr. Johnson enjoys reading, poetry, painting, and music. You may contact Dr. Johnson by using the information listed below.

Other Info

Mailing/Postal Info:

Eduka Solutions
330 W. Main St #214
Middletown, PA 17057

Electronic Address:

E-mail Address: benwoodpost@gmail.com

Other Info:

Find the author (Ben Wood Johnson) on the following media platforms.

Official Twitter handle: @benwoodpost

Official Facebook Page: @benwoodpost

Websites:

Official blog (Ben Wood Post): www.benwoodpost.org

Official website: www.drbenwoodjohnson.com

Academic website: www.benwoodjohnson.com

You may sign up to receive regular updates about the author's academic activities

Other Works

Other works by Dr. Ben Wood Johnson include the following:

- Racism: What is it?

- Sartrean Ethics: A Defense of Jean-Paul Sartre as a Moral Philosopher

- Jean-Paul Sartre and Morality: A Legacy Under Attack

- Sartre Lives On

- Forced Out of Vietnam: A Policy Analysis of the Fall of Saigon

- Natural Law: Morality and Obedience

- Cogito Ergo Philosophus

- Le Racisme et le Socialisme: La Discrimination Raciale dans un Milieu Capitaliste

- International Law: The Rise of Russia as a Global Threat

- Être Noir: Quel Malheur!

- L'homme et le Racisme: Être Responsable de vos Actions et Omissions

- Pennsylvania Inspired Leadership : A Roadmap for American Educators

- Adult Education in America: A Policy Assessment of Adult Learning

- Striving to Survive: The Human Migration Story

TESKO